14.98

AMERICA'S GUIDING LIGHTS

AMERICA'S GUIDING LIGHTS

A *Lighthouse Sketchbook*

Philip C. Ziegler

Technical and Historical Consultants
Kenneth Black and Robert Davis
Shore Village Museum,
Rockland, Maine

DOWN EAST BOOKS

ISBN 0-89272-271-1
Library of Congress Catalog Card Number 89-50889
Book Design by Dawn Peterson
Printed in the United States of America

2   4   5   3   1

Down East Books
Camden, Maine

This book is dedicated to the United States
Coast Guard and to the hundreds of lighthouse
keepers for their undying dedication to assuring
the safe passage of all vessels approaching
America's shores.

CONTENTS

PREFACE

Many years ago, I had the opportunity to sit beside the inlet south of Maine's Portland Head Light with my canvas, paints, and brushes. As I was creating my painting of that most dramatic lighthouse, I fell in love with lighthouses. That love affair eventually led to the writing and illustrating of this book.

With literally hundreds of lighthouses dotting America's coastline from Maine to Hawaii, I was faced with the dilemma of choosing which to include in *America's Guiding Lights*. After over a year spent just gleaning all of the lighthouse information available from every source I could think of, I was deluged by hundreds of photographs and information about my correspondents' "favorite" lighthouses. I immediately established the criteria the lights represented in this book would have to meet: beauty, uniqueness, and historic significance. The illustrations between these covers reflect my personal choices.

I hope and pray that this collection will dispel forever the notion that "once you've seen one lighthouse, you've seen them all." And from those whose own favorite lighthouse does not appear on these pages, I beg forgiveness.

ACKNOWLEDGMENTS

I wish to thank Dr. Robert Scheina, Historian at the United States Coast Guard Headquarters in Washington, D.C., for loaning me many photographs on which to base the illustrations for this book. And thanks to Mr. Frank Beard, of the Maine Historic Preservation Commission; to Mr. Walter Nebiker, of the Rhode Island Historic Preservation Commission; to Sandy Wood, whose photos of California lighthouses were invaluable; and especially to Mr. Colin Mackenzie, Director of the Nautical Research Centre in Petaluma, California, who was always there to dig out those small bits of information I couldn't seem to find anywhere else. I also wish to thank the many state historic commissions and the commanding officers of the district offices of the United States Coast Guard. Without the help of all these individuals, this book could never have been written.

The illustrations and thumbnail histories in *America's Guiding Lights* are based on the materials turned up during my research, and although I make no claims as to the absolute accuracy of the information, I do accept full responsibility for the contents of the book.

A BRIEF HISTORY OF AMERICA'S LIGHTHOUSES

Most of America's lighthouses and other aids to navigation possess integrity of location, design, setting, materials, and workmanship, as well as significant historical associations with their specific localities. These lighthouses not only mark irregular depths near shores, they also indicate the locations of those harbors at whose entrances they stand and the navigational paths into them. Perhaps better than any other class of structure, lighthouses highlight the scenic qualities of the coast and reflect a state's maritime heritage. Lighthouses and their complexes often are associated with specific persons and events and reflect important advances in technology and engineering. Many of these points will be discussed later as the histories are presented of the individual lighthouses that are here portrayed.

From early Colonial times, much of America's history and economy have been interwoven with the sea. Inland farmers and manufacturers exported their respective goods, fishermen harvested the deeper waters and shellfish flats, merchant shipowners traded their goods the world over. Because these activities were complicated by the hazardous character of the coastline and by dangerous storms and fogs, lighthouses and other aids to navigation, such as foghorns and bells, became crucial in developing and maintaining this large-scale economy.

It should be mentioned here that early in its history Massachusetts was the first landfall from Europe, as well as the recognized focus of colonial coastwise trade. Vessels sailing into Boston from the colonies south of the city had to traverse Vineyard and Nantucket sounds and then round the arm of Cape Cod into Boston Harbor. Boats often would have to lie in the sound for weeks while waiting for a favorable westerly wind. During the seventeenth and early eighteenth centuries, fishermen and shipowners constructed crude wooden towers that supported pitch-burning signal lights to mark particularly dangerous waters. The first two formally authorized lighthouses in the Colonies were the Boston Light, erected on Little Brewster Island in 1716, and Brant Point Light, erected on Nantucket Island in 1746.

As was the custom in early Colonial times, these lights were authorized by the general courts. Engineers, architects, and craftsmen, as well as the lighthouse keepers, were hired locally.

The Revolutionary War interrupted most trade, but it did not completely halt maritime traffic or lessen the Colonies' dependence on the sea. After the war, the newly organized federal government realized that navigational aids were necessities and quickly took over their operation. On August 7, 1789, Congress passed an act that created a lighthouse establishment and placed all responsibility for lighthouses under the Treasury Department, where it was to remain until the early twentieth century. Although the responsibility for lighthouses remained within the Treasury Department, supervising officials and designations were changed several times. Secretary of the Treasury Alexander Hamilton placed the lighthouse establishment under the commissioner of revenue in 1792, but in 1802 the new secretary, Albert Gallitin, resumed direct control. However, from 1813 to 1820 the establishment again was placed under the control of the commissioner of revenue and then under that of the fifth auditor of the treasury, Stephen Pleasonton.

Secretary Pleasonton, a dyed-in-the-wool penny pincher, had no maritime experience whatever, and therefore had no true means of even slightly understanding the technological needs of the lighthouses then existing. He relied heavily, as politicians are wont to do, on the advice given to him by friends whose main interest seemed to be personal gain. Such a friend was Winslow Lewis, a manufacturer of an Argand-type lamp, who immediately saw to it that his lamp was installed in the nation's lighthouses.

During the period of Pleasonton's supervision, all lighthouse supplies had to be issued on his personal orders. Although Congress had appropriated money for more lighthouses and illuminating devices, little was actually spent because of Pleasonton's desire to make a name for himself as a great saver of government funds by returning to the Treasury most of the money appropriated for lighthouses each year. As a result of these shenanigans, the deteriorating condition of the lighthouses became a nightmare for mariners, and many ships and hundreds of lives were lost in consequence.

Congress finally saw the light and in 1837 formed a Board of Navy Commissioners whose duty it was to oversee all lighthouse expenditures. Congress then divided the Atlantic Coast into six lighthouse districts and created another two for the Great Lakes, with each district in the charge of a naval officer. The following year the Treasury Department hired a civil engineer, I.W.P. Lewis, to inspect all lighthouses on the New England coast. This marked the first time that a truly qualified engineer was used in any capacity in association with the lighthouse establishment. Although Lewis was the nephew of Pleasonton's friend Winslow Lewis, he honestly decried the deteriorating condition of the lighthouses, their poor administration, and their completely outdated technology. At this point Pleasonton's thirty-two-year hold on the establishment began to crumble. Although ample room for criticism of Pleasonton exists, the fact does remain that during his tenure the number of United States lighthouses grew from fifty-nine in 1820 to 297 by 1850.

It soon became obvious that a determined effort was underway to improve the lighthouse system as new methods of construction and illumination were introduced. The most important development in the history of United States lighthouses was to come in October 1852, when the nine-member Lighthouse Board was established to administer the system for the next fifty-eight years. Congress had finally taken positive action commensurate with the importance of the lighthouse system.

The action proved to be very successful. One of the first acts of the board was to redivide the entire coast of the United States into twelve lighthouse districts, each of which was soon assigned an inspector (naval officer) and an engineer (army officer). But its most significant early accomplishment was the immediate introduction of the Fresnel lens. The board's first report culminated in a 760-page document that detailed the successes and failures of the system as it then existed. During the next ten years great strides were made in lighthouse improvements, and many experiments were made with different fuels, lenses, horns, whistles, and bells.

By the early twentieth century the United States had, unarguably, the finest navigational warning system in the world. By then nineteen lighthouse districts had been established. To administer this huge agency, the Lighthouse Board was transferred from the Treasury Department to the Department of Commerce and Labor in 1903. In 1910, it was reorganized as the Bureau of Lighthouses.

George R. Putnam was selected by President Taft to head this new bureau. In his twenty-five years as commissioner, the bureau grew at an impressive rate, and by 1924 he ran the largest and most efficient lighthouse system in the world. It was responsible for more than 16,800 aids to navigation with more automatic equipment than any other lighthouse system in existence. The use of electrified and automated equipment allowed Putnam to double the number of navigational aids and still remain within his budget. Putnam retired in 1934, and under the Presidential Reorganization Act of 1939, the Bureau of Lighthouses was terminated and then incorporated into the United States Coast Guard, where it remains today. This move transferred the jurisdiction of the lighthouse system back to the Treasury Department, and a full circle was completed.

Gradually the Coast Guard has sold or given away old lighthouses as they have become obsolete—to private citizens or to the Department of the Interior—in order to cut administrative costs and properly maintain those lighthouses that are still active. New methods have led to increasing automation, more efficient lights, and even closed-circuit television that "patrols" the waters from lighthouse towers. The Coast Guard has carried on the efficient and progressive services to mariners that were begun by the Lighthouse Board.

ARCHITECTURE

The first light towers in America were constructed in the eighteenth century, but numbered only twelve by 1790. Early nineteenth-century towers were of moderate height—twenty to fifty feet—and of simple design. Most were strategically placed and their locations were limited to fairly accessible sites easily built upon. Their design was pretty standard, and they were usually entered through a covered walkway that connected directly to the lighthouse-keeper's dwelling.

The towers were constructed of wood or stone and rested on relatively shallow foundations. Where the foundation was built on sand, twelve-by-twelve-foot timber grillage, supported on closely placed piles, was laid in a pit just below water level. A stone rubble base was built on this foundation, directly surmounted by the tower.

A screw-pile structure was an alternative foundation type for sandy areas and was first used in the United States in 1850. Large iron piles fitted with broad-bladed screws were bored down into the sand. The broad screws both furnished increased bearing surface and facilitated driving the piles into the sand.

In closely packed soils such as clay, a shallow excavation was made and a rubble foundation was placed directly within it. On natural rock, loose stones were removed and the surface was made as level as possible. If this could not be done, a foundation step was built to accommodate the rest of the tower.

For a submarine foundation, the builders might make use of a caisson—in effect, an air-filled working-chamber that was lowered deeper and deeper as work-men dug away at the bottom sediments to lay the foundation for the lighthouse. (In the Coast Guard archives, "caisson" also refers to a preformed mold that is sunk to the bottom and then filled with concrete to form the foundation, as at the Borden Flats Light in Fall River, Massachusetts, featured later in this book.)

Wooden towers were constructed of thick first-quality timbers with posts and girths of equal length. The tops of the towers were domed over, and the domes were sheathed with copper flashing. The lantern itself was set on this base, and balcony posts were then attached. The exterior was shingled or clapboarded and was usually given three coats of paint.

Stone towers were usually constructed with walls three feet thick at the base, and in the case of exposed locations, they were over six feet thick. This construction required a much more substantial foundation than was provided for the wooden towers.

Brick towers began to supplant those made of wood or stone by the late eighteenth century, but it was not until the mid nineteenth century that a major change in lighthouse construction began to take place with the introduction of cast-iron structures in the 1840s, skeletal towers by the 1870s, and cast-iron drum towers that could be prefabricated in many sizes. This standardized and relatively cheap type of construction, along with the increase in need, was responsible for the huge increase in the number of light towers after the mid nineteenth century.

In all cases, the tower consisted of three parts that were distinct in their form and were arranged vertically. The bottom element was the shaft, which contained the stairs and formed the greatest part of the tower, varying in size according to the height needed for the location. The clockworks were located in the lamp room, which often appeared to be a continuation of the shaft but was sometimes (especially in primary lights) distinguished by a secondary balcony. This area contained cupboards for parts storage and was used as a general repair area and watch room. The uppermost element of the structure was the lens room, or lantern. This room was distinguished by its large windows and a balcony, which was needed for frequent cleaning of the windows due to the smudge from oil on the inside and salt spray on the outside. The entrance door was made of weather-resistant materials, sometimes iron, more often heavily painted wood—the iron doors being used where the tower was also constructed of iron.

The larger towers often had a gable-roofed entry house, but when they were attached to the keeper's dwelling, they were entered by a covered walkway. These were usually of brick or wood—or of iron, on iron towers. The floors were usually constructed of the same material as the towers. The inner walls of wooden towers were sometimes covered with plaster over laths, and brick was normally used in iron towers. Many towers were not lined at all.

Windows in the earlier towers were not uniform in their overall size or in the panes they contained. In general, windows tended to be small because, although not impossible, it was still difficult to manufacture large panes of glass. In most cases the size of the windows diminished as the height of the tower increased. Some towers that were exposed to vigorous attacks by the elements had a second set of interior windows as storm protection, and many were even equipped with shutters of solid wood or iron.

Staircases were often the most elaborately detailed element within a lighthouse. In wooden towers they tended to be made of wood, and the craftsmen who built them often tried to outdo their contemporaries by making the staircases as fancy as their imaginations would allow. The stairways in cast-iron towers tended to be made of cast iron, although sturdy iron pipe was also used in many cases.

A major feature of every lighthouse was the stove that was required to heat the oil for the lamp in cold weather, but sometimes the oil was so cold it had to be preheated in the kitchen before it would pour. The stove also provided some modicum of comfort for the keeper as he trimmed the wicks of the lamps and generally maintained them.

In general, the exteriors of lighthouse roofs consist of cast-iron sections shaped to conform with the shape of the dome, which were sometimes hexagonal and sometimes octagonal or even round, and all have a ventilating ball at their top to which a copper lightning ground is attached. In most instances the roofs, better known as cupolas, were painted black, although photographs show that other colors have also been used.

Most lighthouses are supplemented by a number of specialized buildings; these include keeper's quarters, covered walkways, oil houses for storage of lamp oil, and various other storage sheds. In addition, in cases where the lighthouses are combined with lifesaving stations, one may find lifeboats, a boathouse, and a structure to house the crews.

The keeper's dwelling, after the tower, was the most important element in a lighthouse complex. In general, these were single-family units, but in some cases multiple-family dwellings were constructed. Much attention was paid to architectural style, and during the Victorian period elaborate jigsaw embellishments were added to dress up what might otherwise be a plain building. Many examples of this Victorian ornamentation can be seen in the illustrations that follow.

THE ATLANTIC COAST

Bass Harbor Head Light, Mt. Desert, Maine

It is difficult to describe the breathtaking beauty of this lighthouse as one approaches it from the sea on a calm, sunny day. I have done my best with my pencil to preserve its loveliness as it sits atop the rocks at the entrance to Blue Hill Bay and Bass Harbor.

Built in 1858, this lighthouse stands like a castle as it shines its light out to sea, and in my opinion it is one of the most picturesque in all America. By land the lighthouse can be reached by traveling from Ellsworth, Maine, along the routes approaching Bar Harbor.

The thousand-pound fog bell that once sounded at the Bass Harbor Head Light is now on display in a small park at the Courier-Gazette building in Rockland, Maine.

Grindle Point Light, Islesboro, Maine

Originally built in 1859, this lighthouse was rebuilt to its present form in 1875 and sold to the town of Islesboro in 1935. It can be approached by ferry from nearby Lincolnville, Maine. It is a beautiful sight when one approaches this lighthouse, one of six square towers built in Maine, and depending on the weather, the lighthouse can be seen from the mainland. A very sturdy and modern ferry landing has been constructed nearby. The keeper's house is now the Sailors' Memorial Museum.

Brown's Head Light, Vinalhaven, Maine

This lighthouse was originally built in 1832 (rebuilt in 1857) on the northeast point of Vinalhaven Island. The keeper's house of the Brown's Head Light is the private residence of the present town manager of Vinalhaven. The island can be reached by ferry from Rockland, Maine.

Goose Rocks Light, Vinalhaven, Maine

When one approaches this lighthouse from the sea, the dangerous rocks and shoals surrounding it are not apparent. Only from the air can one truly see how dangerous this area is for mariners.

Of caisson construction, the Goose Rocks Light was built in 1890 between Vinalhaven and North Haven islands. It marks the eastern entrance of the Fox Islands Thorofare. Known locally by the nickname "The Spark Plug," this was one of the first major lights to use solar power.

The steel canopy pictured surrounding the lower part of the lighthouse has since been removed to ease maintenance problems. It was originally installed to provide shade for the keeper and to catch rain water.

Pemaquid Point Light, Muscongus Bay, Maine

Located on the western side of the bay, this lighthouse was constructed in 1827 and rebuilt in its present form in 1857. It is on a rock foundation surrounded by tillable land, and the keepers were expected to garden there to supply themselves with fresh produce. The dramatic rock formations surrounding this lighthouse show the devastation caused by high waves and glacial wear.

In spite of this warning light, several ships have met their end on the rocks and shoals off Pemaquid. Although the light is still active, the site also contains a small but interesting nautical museum, known as the Fisherman's Museum. A parking lot and picnic area have been built nearby.

Cuckolds Light, Boothbay Harbor, Maine

When an aid to navigation was first planned for this location in 1892, it was decided that a fog signal would be adequate to warn mariners off the rocks upon which the signal was to be built. However, it was soon realized that a real light was needed, so in 1907 a light tower was constructed on top of the fog signal house, which was also the keeper's dwelling.

This complex is built on small, windswept Cuckolds Island about a mile off the tip of Southport Island, out from the village of Newagen. Much marine traffic enters Boothbay Harbor, which in itself is treacherous to navigate, and this light has proved to be a very important aid to navigation in the area.

Halfway Rock Light, Casco Bay, Maine

This sturdy stone lighthouse was constructed in 1877 on a rocky and very treacherous three-acre site, and it was considered one of the most difficult lighthouses to land on in a small boat. It is strategically located in an extremely busy shipping lane.

Supporting the light at first was a huge bell, used when the fog obscured the light. This bell was replaced by a foghorn, but finally that too was discontinued.

The name of this lighthouse probably comes from the fact that it is about halfway between Cape Elizabeth and Small Point, which are at opposite ends of the bay.

High as it is on the rock, much of the Halfway Rock lighthouse was destroyed during a tremendous storm in 1972; severe damage was done to the light itself. But repairs have been made, and today the light remains a very important aid to navigation.

Portland Head Light, Portland, Maine

When America's lighthouses became the responsibility of the federal government in the 1790s, the rate of construction increased rapidly along the New England coast, starting with Maine's first lighthouse, at Portland Head. It was the first light authorized by George Washington and the first erected by the United States government.

The lighthouse was already partially completed in 1790, when Congress appropriated an additional $1,500 toward its final construction, and in 1791 the light was activated. In 1865 the height of the lighthouse was increased by twenty-one feet when its fourth-order Fresnel lens was replaced with a second-order lens. It was lowered again in 1883, then rebuilt to the greater—and final—height two years later.

The Portland Head light is beautifully maintained and remains a bright jewel on Maine's coastline. It is also one of the most photographed American lighthouses.

Spring Point Ledge Light, South Portland, Maine

This illustration shows Spring Point Ledge light as it was originally built about 900 feet from land. In 1951 a breakwater was added between the light and the shore.

This was one of sixty-five caisson-type lighthouses built in the United States, nearly all of which had no accommodation for families. The living quarters for the keeper, such as they were, were located in the area just above the caisson base, surrounded by a protective railing.

Although lighthouses of caisson construction were ostensibly built "to last a lifetime," most such lights on the disused list have rusted so badly that they are now unsafe. As with any other type of construction, they were good only as long as they were well maintained. This lighthouse remains in very good condition and continues to serve as an important beacon.

Cape Neddick Light, York Beach, Maine

From the air, one can clearly see that this lighthouse sits on The Nubble, a seemingly isolated rock island. However, it is actually so close to the shore that at one time visitors were permitted to wade to the island during low tide. (This is no longer allowed.)

The Cape Neddick light is a tourist mecca, and when waves are crashing against the shore, it is a photographer's delight. It has the only red oil house at any lighthouse complex. When the Coast Guard changed color regulations and the building was painted white, the public made such a stir that the Coast Guard capitulated and authorized it to be repainted red. The forty-one-foot light tower was built at the north end of York Beach in 1879, and it is still a very important aid to navigation. The complex includes the keeper's dwelling and auxiliary buildings.

Boon Island Light, York, Maine

Between 1811 and 1830 a great emphasis was placed on erecting a series of lighthouses in the York, Maine area; one of these was the Boon Island Light.

This light was very tall compared to others built during the period. The original lighthouse, first operated in 1812, was seventy feet tall, but because of the importance of its location, the Lighthouse Board considered it too short for a first-class lighthouse. In January 1855, a new stone tower 133 feet high was dedicated. The lighthouse functions as a coastal light and guides vessels to Portsmouth Harbor.

Sitting on a rocky island about six miles from shore, the Boon Island light stands out as one of the loneliest of the many lighthouses that dot the coast of Maine. It was this island that gave its name to a wonderful book written by Kenneth Roberts.

Portsmouth Light, New Hampshire

The original wooden lighthouse was built on Fort Point, a one-and-a-half-acre site on Great Island at the entrance to the Piscataqua River. It survived the rigors of the Revolutionary War, but by 1804 this tower had deteriorated to the point that it needed replacing. A new wooden octagonal tower was built on the same site. This was then replaced in 1877 with an iron tower a short distance from the original site. The focal plane of its flashing light is fifty-two feet above sea level and can be seen for about thirteen miles.

Annisquam Harbor Light, Gloucester, Massachusetts

This lighthouse, originally built in 1801 and rebuilt in 1897, is located on the western side of Wigwam Point near the village of Annisquam, which is a part of the town of Gloucester. The light helps to protect mariners from the long series of sandbars and rocky shoals along the eastern side of the north entrance to the Annisquam River.

This illustration only shows the lighthouse and a portion of the walkway, but beyond this are a keeper's dwelling, a garage, an oil house, and a sea wall.

The tower itself is white-painted brick, cylindrical, and forty-one feet high, with a stone foundation. Residents of Annisquam have free use of the land and beach surrounding the property, which is owned by the Coast Guard. In 1971 the Coast Guard automated the light, which is visible for fifteen miles at sea.

Boston Light, Boston Harbor, Massachusetts

This light, located on Little Brewster Island, marks the main shipping entrance to the harbor. It is effective as a daymarker as well as a nighttime aid, and it is one of the few manned Coast Guard stations in Massachusetts.

The tower, America's first light, was built in 1716. It was blown up by the British in 1776 and rebuilt in 1783. Many other structures have been added to the complex, including a lighthouse entryway in 1783, a keeper's dwelling in 1884, an oil house, and two storage houses that contain the fog signal and a boathouse. One keeper's dwelling was razed in 1960, but a single dwelling remains.

Minots Ledge Light, Boston, Massachusetts

Minots Ledge Light is nicknamed "the lover's light" because of its characteristic flash pattern: 1 (I) — **4** (L-O-V-E) — **3** (Y-O-U), as in the lyrics of a 1916 popular song, "when the lighthouse sends the message 1-4-3. . . ."

The first Minots Ledge Light was built on the outermost Cohasset Rocks twenty miles southeast of Boston in 1850. It was the first lighthouse built in the United States that was completely exposed to the ocean elements. It was constructed of iron piles sunk deeply into the rocks. A small keeper's dwelling was perched high on the open pilings, and on top of that was the light. In March 1851 a severe storm shook the structure so badly the keeper could not go about his duties. This incident loosened the entire structure, and a month later another storm battered the lighthouse so severely that by April 17 nothing was left but some ugly steel pilings jutting from the water. The keeper had gone ashore previous to the second storm, but two assistants perished.

There was no doubt in anyone's mind that a new and sturdier lighthouse was needed, and in 1855 a stone tower was begun. The first forty feet formed a solid base; another forty feet above that housed the working parts of the lighthouse, as well as a keeper's quarters. (The keeper's family was quartered on shore.)

While the new tower was being built, a lightship was anchored at the site to take over the duties of the destroyed lighthouse. The new Minots Ledge light began active duty in November, 1860; it has survived every storm since it was built and it is now fully automated.

Scituate Light, Massachusetts

Sited on Cedar Point at the entrance to Scituate Harbor, this light controls a very important part of the approach to Boston Harbor and has been the site of a great many shipwrecks.

First built in 1811, this octagonal stone lighthouse had a superstructure added in 1827. The lighthouse, keeper's dwelling, oil house, and a well were built at a cost of $3,200. Scituate Light was lit for the last time on November 14, 1860. The very next day the Minots Ledge lighthouse was activated.

Although no longer active, Scituate Light remains a very good example of an early masonry tower of the unusual octagonal form. It is still of great importance for its scenic qualities, with its attached, shingled keeper's dwelling. The town frequently uses it in its public-relations activities.

Race Point Light, Provincetown, Massachusetts

A rubble stone tower was originally built on this site in 1816, and a fog bell was installed thirty-six years later. The tower was rebuilt in 1863 and shingled over. A more powerful light was installed in 1874—along with a steam whistle used when fog was a hazard—and the keeper's dwelling was enlarged.

In 1876 a new tower, illustrated here, was built using cast-iron rings lined with bricks. The complex was electrified in 1957, one of the keeper's dwellings was demolished, and the remaining dwelling was completely modernized.

Cape Cod (Highland) Light, Truro, Massachusetts

Constructed in 1798, this lighthouse, near the town of Truro, was the first such light on Cape Cod. The plane of the light was 160 feet above sea level. The tower was rebuilt in 1833 and again in 1857.

Inasmuch as this light was usually the first sighted by traffic from Europe to Massachusetts, a Fresnel lens—the most modern light obtainable—was installed in 1857. This comparatively short tower is located so that its light is now 183 feet above the sea. It is one of the most important lights in the area.

Three Sisters of Nauset (The Beacon) Eastham, Massachusetts

Originally, three lighthouses stood on Nauset Beach. Their lights were fixed in order to differentiate them from the single towers in the area. Built of brick, these structures were erected too close to the water on the sandy beach; erosion gradually reduced them to nothing but brick foundations. They were replaced with three wooden towers atop the bluff. Two of these structures were eventually sold to private buyers. From an artist's point of view the one remaining is truly beautiful. It is a wood-frame, two-story tower built in 1892; the one-story dwelling was attached in 1923.

The National Park Service acquired this property in February 1975; as of 1981 plans were being made to move this complex to another site to be completely restored.

Chatham Light, Massachusetts

This Coast Guard lifeboat station is on the west side of Chatham Harbor on a bluff overlooking the inlet and Nauset Bear Sand Bar. It is at the "elbow" of Cape Cod that divides Nantucket Sound from the open sea. Its light is for the benefit of ships approaching Monomoy Point and Pollock Rip Shoals.

Built in 1877, this forty-eight-foot cast-iron tower had a "twin" that has since been removed to Nauset Beach. The structure to the left of the light is built on a base of structural steel and is used as a supplemental lookout and to accommodate additional equipment.

A Federal-style garage was added in 1937, and major additions have bben made to the keeper's dwelling, which had most of its windows replaced in 1950. In 1981 plans were approved to build a barracks on the site. Since this illustration was rendered, a much larger lantern has been added.

Great Point Light, Nantucket, Massachusetts

Forty acres of remote, undeveloped land surround this lighthouse, which is in a wildlife preserve on the northerly tip of Nantucket Island. Built on the first Nantucket landfall seen from the ocean, the light guides ships away from Cross Rip and Tuckernuck Shoals.

Initially, navigators confused the Nantucket light with the Cross Rip lightship, and there were several ships wrecked in the area. Slow to respond, the Lighthouse Board finally had the light altered in 1889 to alleviate the confusion.

The original lighthouse, built on the site in 1784, was made of wood and was destroyed by fire in 1816. A second lighthouse, illustrated here, was constructed in 1818 of rubble stone. Later fully automated, it was an important lighthouse until it was destroyed in a severe storm in March 1984. It has since been rebuilt to look like the previous light—at a cost of over two million dollars.

Brant Point Light, Nantucket, Massachusetts

Two previous lighthouses existed on the site before a third was constructed just before the Revolution. Although it survived the war, it burned to the ground in 1783. It was succeeded by a fourth and inferior light and then by a fifth—thought to be much stronger than the previous lights—which simply blew down in a storm two years later.

At that point the government took over and built a much more substantial light tower atop the keeper's dwelling. However, by 1853 this light had deteriorated and needed replacing. A brick tower was built on the site in 1856, but soon the channel into Nantucket Harbor shifted to the point that this light became useless. The present lighthouse, illustrated here, was constructed in a more effective location, and although, at twenty feet, it is New England's lowest light, its effectiveness has been proved over the ensuing years.

A replica of this light is on display at Mystic Seaport Museum.

Nobska Point Light, Woods Hole, Massachusetts

This lighthouse is a major navigational aid located at the entrance to Woods Hole Harbor between Buzzard's Bay and Vineyard Sound. Its light can be seen from any direction.

Originally built in 1829 and rebuilt in 1876, this is an excellent example of a typical lighthouse complex, with the keeper's dwelling and outbuildings built adjacent to the tower. The lighthouse, which is floodlit from sunset to sunrise, is picturesquely situated on a bluff overlooking Vineyard Sound. In 1948 a skeletal tower was added to accommodate a radio beacon.

Gay Head Light, Martha's Vineyard, Massachusetts

This was the first lighthouse constructed on Martha's Vineyard; it was lighted in 1799. Located on the western tip of the island, it was an octagonal wooden structure built on a stone foundation. The tower itself was only forty-seven feet high, but because of its elevated location, the plane of the flashing light was 160 feet above sea level.

The lighthouse deteriorated to the point that the Lighthouse Board decided to build a replacement, illustrated here. It was put into service in December 1856, and the light could be seen from nineteen miles at sea. The light was constructed adjacent to and centered in front of a double keeper's dwelling that was much like the duplexes of today. It still functions both as a seacoast light and a guide to the entrance to Martha's Vineyard. However, the keeper's dwelling was no longer standing as of 1904.

Borden Flats Light, Fall River, Massachusetts

Of caisson construction, this light station was built in 1881. The light itself is made of brick and cement. It is located on a reef at the mouth of the Taunton River, which is also a part of Fall River. Although it is not shown in the illustration, the Braga Bridge (Interstate 195) passes almost directly above the lighthouse.

To construct the light, a cast-iron cylindrical shell was sunk firmly and secured with cement to the reef, which is located about midpoint in the river. This shell was then filled with fifteen feet of concrete. This constitutes the foundation, which is primarily below sea level. The superstructure houses the keeper's quarters and work space, surmounted by the light.

In 1957 the entire structure was electrified, having been previously run on oil, and in 1963 the light was automated. The brass bell, over one hundred years old, was still in operation in 1981. Today, the complex is beautifully maintained by the Coast Guard.

Stonington Harbor Light, Connecticut

First built in 1824 on Windmill Point, the lighthouse was relocated to the east side of Stonington Harbor in 1840, where it served until Stonington Breakwater Light was established in 1889. This lovely old lighthouse was then moved from its original site to the town of Stonington, where the structure is now preserved by the local historical society.

Much credit must be given to the hundreds of such local historical societies for the wonderful work they are doing by preserving thousands of all types of historical structures throughout the United States.

New London Harbor Light and New London Ledge Light, Connecticut

Although the mouth of the Thames River at New London forms a fine natural harbor, many dangerous shoals and ledges present a serious hazard to marine traffic. A daybeacon was strategically placed at the entrance of this harbor about 1750, but it proved to be very inefficient. (The Coast Guard Light List defines daybeacons as "unlighted fixed aids to navigation . . . identified by their color and the shape of the daymark.")

In 1760 New London Harbor Light, a stone tower, was constructed to replace the beacon. Funds were raised through a lottery, which was a common means used in many communities during the mid 1700s to raise funds for building churches.

This light had stood only thirty-nine years when it began to deteriorate. It was replaced by a new stone tower (first illustration) in 1801, and although New London Harbor Light still stands, the New London Ledge Light (second illustration) was added in 1908–09. It was built on a very dangerous ledge, and as the illustration shows, it is sturdy and elaborately built.

Bullock's Point Light, Narragansett Bay (East Providence), Rhode Island

Built in 1872, this architecturally significant structure was demolished in 1939 after severe hurricane damage. Although now gone, this lovely lighthouse deserves a place in this book.

Pomham Rocks Light, East Providence, Rhode Island

This lighthouse is unique for its rugged, romantic setting on Pomham Rocks, only about one hundred feet from shore. It was built in 1871. The dwelling and the oil house dominate this tiny three-quarter-acre "island." It is an impressive sight, contrasting with the oil tanks on the western shore and the architecture of the small light station that guides vessels up the narrow Providence River Channel. The sight of the rocks and the small, yet detailed, nineteenth-century architecture of this lighthouse complex gives a nice impression of Rhode Island lighthouses.

Conimicut Light, Narragansett Bay, Rhode Island

The original wooden daybeacon at Conimicut Point was built in 1857. A vane on top of a spindle pointed in the direction of the channel that led to Providence. A granite tower was built to replace the old wooden beacon, and then a cast-iron structure (illustrated here) was built nearby in 1868.

For a time the only accommodation for the keeper was in the granite tower, and he had to use a boat to get to the new cast-iron light. In 1874 a new keeper's dwelling was built near the granite tower, but in the same year it was demolished by a heavy field of floating ice coming down the Providence River channel. The keeper moved into an old abandoned dwelling until the cast-iron tower was fitted with living quarters.

The light was electrified in 1960, the last one in the country to be so equipped.

Beavertail Light, Jamestown, Rhode Island

Located on Conanicut Island at the tip of Beavertail Point, this lighthouse is an important guide to ships at the point where the Atlantic Ocean meets busy Narragansett Bay. A beacon was established here in Colonial times and was known as Newport or Conanicut Light, making this the oldest lighthouse site on the Rhode Island coast. A rubble stone tower was built in 1749, the third official lighthouse erected on the entire Atlantic Coast. The foundation of this lighthouse remains, and a historical marker recalls its background. The present granite tower was erected in 1856.

Beavertail Light was closely associated with the testing and development of fog signals; many new types were tested here before being generally adopted at other lighthouses. The light has been automated and is not manned by the Coast Guard.

North Light, Block Island, Rhode Island

This lighthouse on Sandy Point, the northern extremity of Block Island not quite five miles from Old Harbor, was erected in 1867. Though now the oldest lighthouse on the island, it was built on the site of three previous structures that, over a thirty-eight-year period, had all been rendered useless by storms and shifting sands. Well built of stone and protected much better than its predecessors, it served for over one hundred years, until it was abandoned as an active lighthouse in 1970.

Point Judith Light, Narragansett, Rhode Island

Point Judith is known to all mariners of the Atlantic Coast. All ships and pleasure craft plying the waters to and from Narragansett Bay and Long Island Sound must "turn this corner." Point Judith's ground swells, when they occur, do not discriminate between large craft and small. The lighthouse juts out from Point Judith and, like others off the Rhode Island coast, is an important light warning sea traffic not to venture too close to the surrounding rocks. During the Revolution a beacon was maintained here, and a Coast Guard station built nearby in 1888 was replaced by the present structure in 1935. The Point Judith lighthouse, built in 1810 and rebuilt in 1857, adjoins the Coast Guard station.

Watch Hill Light, Westerly, Rhode Island

In 1806 the United States government acquired the land upon which this lighthouse was built. The light was first lit in 1808. The first building on this site was a round wooden tower with shingle siding. In 1858 it was replaced by the present brick-and-granite structure and tower. Watch Hill Light is automatically operated and is located in an area noted for excellent surf fishing. It overlooks miles of Rhode Island's famous ocean resort beaches.

Southeast Light, Block Island, Rhode Island

One of the most important lighthouses on the Atlantic Coast, this light can be seen for thirty-five miles. Built in 1874, it stands on top of the Monhegan Bluffs, two hundred feet above sea level. The structure itself is a two-and-one-half-story brick building, and the octagonal tower rises fifty-two feet above its base.

Off Southeast Light are the world's best bluefin tuna fishing grounds, and world-record bluefish and striped bass have been taken by surf fishermen off Block Island.

A great threat to the existence of this lighthouse is the force of the sea eroding—at the rate of thirty inches per year—the clay bluffs upon which it is built. Plans are being made to move the lighthouse back from the bluffs; it will cost about one million dollars, which will be raised through private donations.

Rock Island Light, Alexandria Bay, New York

Built in 1882, this lighthouse is one of a complex of six buildings constructed on a four-acre outcropping in the Thousand Islands area of the St. Lawrence River near the town of Alexandria Bay. It replaced a primitive lantern established in 1848.

Although it has been removed from active service, Rock Island Light is now maintained by the state of New York as an example of such self-sufficient facilities once common along the St. Lawrence River.

The Statue of Liberty, New York, New York

Without a doubt the most famous lighthouse in the United Sates is the Statue of Liberty. Built in France as a memorial to independence, the statue was formally presented by the French to the United States ambassador in Paris on July 4, 1884. It was then disassembled, crated, and shipped to the United States. Although it no longer functions as a lighthouse, the statue, then known as "Liberty Enlightening the World," was originally lighted by nine electric arc lamps within the torch. These were first lighted on November 22, 1886. The light was 302 feet above the sea and was visible for twenty-four miles.

After the statue had served fifteen years of active duty as a lighthouse, the Lighthouse Board extinguished its light and turned it over to the War Department. Due to local pressure, they maintained the light for several more years. The statue is now part of the National Park system. More than two million visitors tour the monument annually.

Fort Tompkins Light, Verrazano Narrows, New York

When the United States Coast Guard Archives loaned me a photograph of this lighthouse, I was truly delighted. Upon finishing the illustration I attempted to ascertain the history of this lighthouse, only to find that not one bit of information seemed to exist pertaining to it. Under such circumstances I would ordinarily put the illustration aside, but feeling that the reader would be just as delighted as I was to see such a structure, I have included it in the book. Only one fact came to light during my research, and that is that this structure was moved to Fort Wadsworth in 1903.

Sandy Hook Light, Sandy Hook, New Jersey

Built in 1764, this is the oldest active light in continuous operation in the United States. It is located at the Gateway National Recreational Area, about twelve miles north of Long Branch, New Jersey. Although threatened by erosion in the late nineteenth century, the problem seems to have been corrected, as this old lighthouse tower has weathered the years gracefully.

Navesink Light, Navesink, New Jersey

Although signal lights warning of the approach of enemy vessels were used on these heights as early as 1746, it was not until 1828 that the government built the twin light towers that marked the western entrance to New York Bay. By 1857 these original towers had deteriorated badly and had to be replaced. Two brownstone towers, one square and one octagonal, connected by an elaborate building, were erected and put into service in 1862.

Navesink Light was the first (in 1883) to use mineral oil as fuel for its lanterns. In 1898 the south tower became the first electrified lighthouse in the United States. The north tower was decommissioned at about the same time. The Coast Guard turned the structure over to the Borough of Highlands, New Jersey, in 1954, and it has been developed into an historic site with an excellent museum displaying a fully operating eleven-foot Fresnel lens.

Barnegat Light, Clam Island, New Jersey

Located on the south side of Barnegat Inlet about forty miles northeast of Atlantic City, this light was inaugurated on July 20, 1835. Within twenty years the mortar had deteriorated, and bricks began falling at an alarming rate. Moreover, the tower was only forty feet high and the light could only be seen for ten miles—in clear weather. So in 1857 construction began on a new tower nine hundred feet south of the old one; its light was 175 feet above the sea. It was lighted on January 1, 1859. This tower was also threatened by erosion, so jetties were built around it. In 1926 the station—excluding the tower—was given to the state of New Jersey. It still stands, and is visited by thousands of tourists every year. The Fresnel lens, which was removed from the light, is on display at the Barnegat Historical Society Museum.

Greenbury Point Light, Annapolis, Maryland

This lighthouse was built in 1849 near the Naval Academy in Annapolis, and its use as a lighthouse was limited because its light was hard to distinguish from those emanating from the Academy. In 1891 the light was extinguished, and the structure was then used as a daybeacon. It was replaced by a screw-pile lighthouse one thousand yards offshore. The old lighthouse is illustrated here because of its beauty and its architectural and historical significance.

Thomas Point Shoal Light, Annapolis, Maryland

Here we have an interesting view from eye level. The original lighthouse at this location was built in 1825 and was torn down and rebuilt in 1838. However, this structure was put out of service in 1845 when a new hexagonal lighthouse was lighted on November 20 of that year. Due to ice damage in 1886, fourteen hundred tons of riprap was placed strategically around the base of the structure. The light—now automated—is forty-three feet above the water and can be seen from thirteen miles away.

Seven Foot Knoll Light, Chesapeake Bay (Baltimore), Maryland

Although donated by the Coast Guard to the city of Baltimore, and now situated at Pier 5 in Baltimore Harbor, this lighthouse was originally located at Newport News, Virginia. It was established in 1855 in eight feet of water off the mouth of the Patapsco River near Baltimore and was the second lighthouse set in open water in Chesapeake Bay to mark the river. It is of screw-pile construction, and the light itself was forty-five feet above water.

Wolf Trap Light, Chesapeake Bay, Maryland

In the 1870s screw-pile lighthouses replaced the lightships at both Wolf Trap and Thimble Shoals in Chesapeake Bay. The Wolf Trap structure was lighted in October 1870. In January 1893 floating ice in the bay tore it from its foundations. It was found floating toward the cape, was towed toward the beach, and finally drifted ashore. The Lighthouse Board replaced the screw-pile structure with a caisson lighthouse (illustrated here) in 1894.

Piney Point Light, Piney Point, Maryland

This light was the first lighthouse built on the Potomac River, although there had been several lightships on the river since 1821. Located on the Maryland side, fourteen miles from the mouth of the Potomac, the lighthouse was built in 1836. It is no longer in operation, although the Coast Guard still maintains a station at Piney Point.

Jones Point Light, Alexandria, Virginia

This small structure was built in 1855, just a half-dozen miles from Washington, D.C., at Jones Point on the Potomac River. It is the oldest standing inland lighthouse. When Washington, Georgetown, and Baltimore began to lose their importance as ports in the early 1900s, it was recommended that Jones Point Light be decommissioned. A steel tower flashing a light was then constructed nearby but was torn down in the late 1930s.

Although this illustration shows the lighthouse in severe disrepair, it has since been restored and is now owned by the National Park Service.

Tangier Sound Light, Chesapeake Bay, Virginia

The superstructure of this lighthouse was torn down in 1961 and replaced by a steel tower of the same height. The original structure was so quaint and lovely that I chose to include it here, feeling that such an architecturally significant building should at least be preserved in memory. It was built at the western side of the entrance to Tangier Sound in 1890 at a cost of $25,000.

Assateague Light, Assateague Island, Virginia

In the early 1830s there was no lighthouse between Chesapeake and Delaware bays, so in 1831 Congress appropriated money to build a lighthouse near the Chincoteague Islands. In 1833 a light tower was built near the Virginia/Maryland border, but it was too low and the light too feeble to be effective, so a new light was begun in 1859. Construction on this light was held up by the Civil War, and work was not resumed until 1865. It was officially lighted on October 1, 1867. The new tower, with its first-order lens, was high enough to be visible for nineteen miles. Though still active, the light is now automated. It is surrounded by the Chincoteague National Wildlife Refuge.

Sandy Point Light, Chesapeake Bay, Virginia

This caisson lighthouse was built in 1897. With a superstructure of brick atop a concrete-filled iron-shell base, the light has withstood the roughest seas nature could fling against it. Other lighthouses constructed of lighter materials at this site were destroyed by the ice and storms. Before the construction of Sandy Point Light, warning was provided by lightships.

Point of Shoals Light, Chesapeake Bay, Virginia

In the ten years just preceding the Civil War, many lighthouses were established in Chesapeake Bay and in rivers emptying into the bay. This lovely jewel of architecture, of typical screw-pile construction, was built in 1855 in the James River. Others built in the area at this time were the Drum Point Light, the light at Fort Washington, and the light at Fort Carroll in Baltimore Harbor. These were all small lights.

Old Point Comfort Light and New Point Comfort Light, Hampton Roads, Virginia

In 1802 Old Point Comfort Light (first illustration) was built at the entrance to Hampton Roads at Old Point Comfort near Fortress Monroe. A second light tower was built in 1805 at New Point Comfort (second illustration) at the entrance to Mobjack Bay. This light was battered during the Civil War but survived. Both light towers still stand essentially as they were originally built.

Pages Rock Light, Yorktown, Virginia

This lighthouse was first lighted on September 20, 1893. It was built on wooden piles driven six feet into the shoal and encased in iron sleeves. The light was forty-one feet above the water. In 1967 this truly beautiful structure was demolished and a small flashing light was installed on the foundation.

Currituck Beach Light, North Carolina

Until 1875 there was a gap of about forty miles of unlighted waters between the Cape Henry and Bodie Island lighthouses on the Outer Banks of North Carolina. Many ships and lives had been lost along this part of the coast as they attempted to avoid entering the Gulf Stream. When Currituck Beach Light was activated on December 1, 1875, its first-order lens, standing 158 feet above sea level, could be seen for nineteen miles, and thus the dark section between Cape Henry and Bodie Island was lighted. In order to distinguish the Currituck Beach lighthouse from other lights on the Outer Banks, the tower was not painted but retained its natural red brick color.

Bodie Island Light, North Carolina

When this lighthouse was constructed in 1848, experts recommended that wooden pilings be driven into the bottom to form a firm foundation. Ignoring this advice, an overseer appointed by the government decided that a double layer of bricks would provide an adequate foundation. Within two years of its completion the tower began to lean toward the east, and despite efforts to straighten it, the tower was soon beyond repair.

In 1859 a new tower was built, this time on a foundation of wooden pilings; its light was ninety feet above sea level. But in 1861 the Confederates set off a charge in the tower that left it in ruins. A third tower, 156 feet high, was built at this location in 1872. Southbound vessels can now safely round Cape Hatteras without entering the Gulf Stream. However, the main purpose of the light is to keep ships clear of Bodie Island.

Cape Hatteras Light, Chesapeake Bay, North Carolina

Probably the most dangerous area for vessels along the southern Atlantic coast is the shallow, rocky finger known as Diamond Shoals. Because the shoals extend out for a distance of eight miles from Cape Hatteras, it was proposed in the 1790s that a lighthouse be built at the end. However, technology was not far enough advanced to allow construction of a lighthouse on such rough terrain amid the terrible storms that plagued the area. Consequently, the site eventually selected was at Cape Hatteras, and a ninety-five-foot tower was constructed there in 1803. The quality of that light was the target of frequent complaints, so in 1854 the height of the tower was increased to 150 feet above sea level and a much stronger light was installed.

The lantern at Cape Hatteras Light was removed by the Confederates at the beginning of the Civil War, but the tower was left intact. Federal troops finally routed the Confederates, and the tower was relighted in 1862. By the end of the Civil War this tower was considered beyond repair, and in 1870 a new lighthouse, illustrated here, was constructed six hundred feet northeast of the old tower. The light was about 190 feet above average low water, making it the tallest brick tower in the country. To make it a better daymark, the tower was painted with black and white spiral stripes.

Because of its age and condition, this tower was replaced in 1936 by a skeleton tower built nearby. Eventually the old lighthouse was turned over to the National Park Service to be included in the Cape Hatteras National Seashore, where it is now a museum.

Cape Lookout Light, near Shackleford Bank, North Carolina

At the point where this lighthouse is located, dangerous shoals protrude for about ten miles out to sea. The light was first activated in 1812, but it was never considered very effective, and in 1859 it was rebuilt with its light 156 feet above sea level and visible for nineteen miles.

The distinctive diamond pattern, painted on the tower to make it more effective as a daymark, resulted in a nearby community being named Diamond City.

Oak Island Light, North Carolina

The Oak Island lighthouse is located on a peninsula between the Elizabeth River and the Atlantic Ocean. It began service on May 19, 1958, replacing the nearby Cape Fear lighthouse. At 169 feet above the water, the light can be seen for nineteen miles. The lighthouse complex, which includes boat docks, a radar tower, an administrative building, and personnel quarters, is operated by the United States Coast Guard.

Cape Romain Light, McClellanville, South Carolina

Lighthouse Island (originally known as Raccoon Key) in the Cape Romain Wildlife Refuge, is the setting for two lighthouses constructed by the United States government—the first in 1827 and its replacement in 1857. With the exception of the Civil War years, the towers provided constant protection from 1827 to 1947 to vessels approaching the Cape Romain Shoals. Of the 1827 lighthouse, only the brick tower remains, divested of its paint and its lamp, as depicted in the background of this illustration.

The 1857 lighthouse, built to replace the inadequate 1827 tower, was first lighted on January 1, 1858. It is 150 feet tall and is octagonal in shape. The focal plane of the light was 161 feet above sea level. The light was discontinued in 1947 and is now a tourist attraction. Due to settling of its foundation, the lighthouse leans about four degrees toward the abandoned tower, though this illustration was drawn at an angle that does not show the tilt.

Charleston (Morris Island) Light, South Carolina

A light tower was built on Morris Island, at the entrance to Charleston Harbor, in 1767. At the end of the Revolutionary War the Tybee light, to the south, and the Charleston light were the only two lighthouses south of Delaware Bay. The Charleston light, unlike many others, survived the Revolution, and in 1790 it was put under the aegis of the federal government. This tower had a revolving light 125 feet above sea level. However, during the Civil War the Confederates destroyed the lamp, and soon thereafter the tower itself was destroyed.

In 1874 the new tower, illustrated here, was built on a concrete foundation eight feet thick. It was made of brick and was 161 feet high. Although damaged severely by a hurricane in 1885 and then by an earthquake in 1886, the tower survived, but it was eventually replaced by the lighthouse on Sullivan's Island—probably the most modern of all light towers built in the United States. The new Charleston light station, built on Sullivan's Island in 1962, has the most powerful beam (twenty-eight million candlepower) in the Western Hemisphere; it is visible for thirty-five miles. The tower is of aluminum construction and boasts an elevator.

Haig's Point Light, Daufuskie Island, South Carolina

Few other lighthouses are as picturesque as Haig's Point Light, built in 1873. It was one of two sets of navigational lights that were constructed on Daufuskie Island. The Haig's Point range lights (also referred to as the Daufuskie Island Lights) operated until 1924. The rear beacon was mounted on the keeper's house and had a fifth-order Fresnel lens. This illustration is based on a photograph provided by the South Carolina Department of Archives and History.

Tybee Island Light, Savannah, Georgia

When General James Oglethorpe founded the Colony of Georgia in 1732, one of his first actions was to erect a lightless tower as a point of reference for vessels entering the waterways of Savannah. It was located about twenty miles inland. This tower was completed in 1736, then destroyed by a hurricane in 1741. Undaunted, Oglethorpe had another light tower constructed, slightly taller than the first, and put a light in it, thus qualifying it as the third true lighthouse built in the United States.

By the time the Revolutionary War began, the tower had seriously deteriorated, and it was replaced by a brick tower in 1773. Although the light was in use when the federal government took jurisdiction over it in 1791, its status as a working lighthouse between 1775 and 1791 is unknown. During the Civil War the Confederates set fire to the interior of the tower. It was subsequently repaired and its height increased to 144 feet. In 1871 the tower was damaged by a severe gale and was condemned by the Lighthouse Board, but Congress never took action on the suggestion that it be replaced. The old tower stands today, a monument to the parsimony of Congress.

THE GULF COAST AND FLORIDA

Cape Canaveral (Cape Kennedy) Light, Florida

Built in 1848, this lighthouse proved to be inadequate, and twenty years later a more efficient one was constructed, with its light 139 feet above sea level. It wasn't long before sea erosion threatened the new tower, and by 1883 only 192 feet of beach separated the lighthouse from the Atlantic Ocean. Attempts to halt this erosion were unsuccessful, and the old tower was demolished and a new one constructed about 1.25 miles to the west in 1894. Now known as the Cape Kennedy Light, it is still active today.

Jupiter Inlet Light, Palm Beach, Florida

This light was first put into operation on July 10, 1860. The following year, the shores of Florida were blockaded by the United States Navy in order to prevent Confederate ships from reaching shore. In August 1861 a group of Confederate sympathizers rendered the light useless by removing the lighting apparatus.

Relighted in 1866, the Jupiter Inlet lighthouse has continued to operate ever since. In 1886 a life-saving station was established on the site. During World War II enemy activities off the coast resulted in a submarine alert in which the lighthouse was involved. American vessels were torpedoed off nearby Hobe Sound in 1942.

Cape Florida Light, Key Biscayne, Florida

As originally constructed, this lighthouse was sixty-five feet high, and although it was supposed to have been made of solid brick walls surrounding a central shaft, some years after its construction it was discovered that the corrupt contractor had built it with hollow walls.

The lighthouse was destroyed and one man killed in an attack by Seminole Indians in 1836. The wounded assistant keeper barricaded himself in the top of the tower and miraculously survived the fire that destroyed the keeper's house and all the wooden portions of the tower itself, including the stairs. He was rescued after being trapped in the burned-out tower for twenty-four hours. Rebuilding of the light was authorized a year after its destruction, but because of continuing harassment by hostile Indians, it was not completed until 1846.

Due to its reputation as a poor light, the tower was raised to ninety-five feet in 1855. Today Cape Florida Light looks much as it did then. Florida's acquisition of the property on which the lighthouse stands insures the preservation of this historic landmark.

Sands Key Light, Florida

First lighted on July 20, 1853, Sands Key Light is the second oldest of the six screw-pile lighthouses that extend from Fowey Rocks to Sands Key. In 1865 a hurricane entirely washed away the island upon which the lighthouse had been built. Since then the island has re-formed, and the Sands Key light is now the only one of the six that does not stand entirely in the water. The tower is situated on part of the land acquired in 1821 through the Adams-Onis Treaty, under the terms of which Spain ceded Florida to the United States.

The original conical tower, completed in 1827, was not so well secured as its present screw-pile replacement. It was undermined by the action of hurricane-driven waves nineteen years after it was built, and the tower and keeper's house collapsed upon their occupants. A lightship served in its place until 1853, at which time the ironwork tower was completed.

Key West Light, Florida

Built in 1825, the original tower of this lighthouse was sixty-five feet tall and was destroyed by a hurricane in 1846 that killed the keeper and his family. It was immediately rebuilt on the same site but five feet shorter than the original tower. Years later an additional twenty feet were added to its height.

When the lighthouse was taken out of service in 1969, the Key West Art and Historical Society got the future use of it as a part of a museum complex that houses military and marine artifacts in the old keeper's house. Note that this illustration depicts the lighthouse as it appeared in 1846.

Garden Key (Dry Tortugas) Light, Fort Jefferson, Florida

In 1825 the Dry Tortugas light tower was built on Garden Key (then called Bush Key) on what was to become the parade ground of Fort Jefferson. But when a new lighthouse was built on Loggerhead Key in 1858, the Dry Tortugas light was moved there, reducing the old tower to a fourth-order harbor light. After a storm damaged the tower in 1876, the light was moved about thirty yards and rebuilt atop a staircase of the fort, as shown here. Although the lighthouse is now severely deteriorated, plans to restore it are underway.

Boca Grande Light, Florida

This lighthouse is located at the southern tip of Gasparilla Island in the Boca Grande Lighthouse Reservation. The light was activated on December 31, 1890, and remained of primary significance until 1960, when the entire lighthouse was moved two miles to the north. It was restored in 1988.

St. Marks Light, Wakulla, Florida

Construction on this lighthouse began in 1829 and was completed in 1831. Reports indicate that limestone blocks used in its construction came from either the nearby ruins of old Fort of San Marcos de Apalache or nearby quarries. Like many lighthouses built during this period, it was located too close to the shore. Realizing the inevitability of its destruction, Fifth Auditor Stephen Pleasonton had it relocated a short distance inland in 1841–42.

During the Civil War, many military skirmishes were conducted in its immediate area. On March 4, 1865, one of the largest efforts launched against the Rebels in the interior of West Florida began with a landing of a thousand federal troops at St. Marks Light.

Supervision of this lighthouse was transferred to the United States Coast Guard in 1939, and although the building itself is not open to the public, the lighthouse is within the St. Marks Wildlife Refuge and is an important tourist attraction.

Crooked River Light, Carrabelle, Florida

A growing lumber trade from the Apalachicola River to Crooked River southwest of Carrabelle prompted the construction of this lighthouse, which replaced the Dog Island lighthouse destroyed in 1873.

The Crooked River lighthouse was first lighted on October 28, 1895. Still active today, the 115-foot-high light is visible for seventeen miles at sea. The tower acts also as a daymark, with the upper half painted dark red and the lower half white.

Pensacola Light, Florida

The original lighthouse on Pensacola Bay was constructed during the fall of 1824 and was lighted on December 20 of that year. However, both the height (eighty feet above sea level) and the strength of the light proved to be unsatisfactory. Although a new lighthouse was proposed in 1837 as part of a scheme to improve the lighting for Pensacola Harbor, it was not until 1859 that a new light was put into service on the bay.

Direct hits by Confederate cannonballs put the light out of service during the Civil War. A first-order light was reestablished in 1869. Many years later, severe cracks were discovered in the tower, caused by the stress of the shelling during the war. They were adequately repaired, and no further problems have occurred.

The two Pensacola lighthouses—the original that served from 1824 to 1859, and the present one—have provided signal and sentinel services for the Pensacola area for almost as long as Florida has been part of the United States.

Biloxi Light, Mississippi

A conical cast-iron tower, this light went into service in 1848. In 1867 it was noted that the tower had begun to lean toward one side, much like the Tower of Pisa. A truly great engineering feat was accomplished when the foundation was dug out on one side and the tower was brought to level. Although painted black in 1867, it was again painted white two years later. No longer an active lighthouse, it remains an important tourist attraction as part of Biloxi City Park.

Cat Island Light, Gulfport, Mississippi

The original lighthouse on Cat Island went into service in 1831, but it was destroyed by the Confederates during the Civil War. Because of the condition of the land, the second lighthouse (shown here) was built on screw piles; it was finished in 1871. Used until 1938, Cat Island Light is no longer standing, but its serene beauty will remain in the minds of those fortunate enough to have seen it.

Point au Fer Light, Eugene Island, Louisiana

The first light station at Point au Fer, on Eugene Island in Atchafalaya Bay, was lighted in 1827. It remained in service until 1859, when its duties were taken over by the Southwest Reef Bay Light. In spite of battering by a storm a few years after its construction, this lighthouse continued to function until shortly after World War I. The third Point au Fer Light (shown here) was constructed in 1916. This illustration depicts the lighthouse as it looked before the Coast Guard burned it to the ground, replacing it with a steel skeleton tower.

Oyster Bayou Light, Atchafalaya Bay, Louisiana

In 1894 the Lighthouse Board recommended that a light station be built at Oyster Bayou to mark the easternmost entrance to Atchafalaya Bay. The lighthouse, completed in 1903, was located in six feet of water. This was a typical dwelling built on piles, with the light, which was forty-seven feet above sea level, sitting atop the structure. It could be seen for seven miles. In 1946 electric power was installed and the light was automated. The original building remains as a daymark.

Southwest Pass Entrance Light, near Port Eads, Louisiana

The tower shown here is the fifth one built to mark the Southwest Pass through the Mississippi delta to the Mississippi River.

The first lighthouse, built in 1831, collapsed in 1838 due to shoddy construction. In the same year a second tower was built, but it deteriorated and later needed to be replaced. The third light built on the site, in 1870, was constructed like a fortress. It had a formidable foundation and an iron superstructure, and the light itself was 128 feet above sea level. This lighthouse still stands—a lonesome derelict.

The third light was eventually replaced by one named the Southwest Pass East Jetty Light, which was built too close to the shipping lanes. It was struck by passing ships so many times that little but the foundation remains today. A fifth lighthouse now marks the pass.

Sabine Pass Light, Louisiana

This brick lighthouse, located at the mouth of the Sabine River, which forms the border between Louisiana and Texas, was completed in 1856. The light was extinguished during the Civil War and reactivated on December 23, 1865. In 1886 a cyclone completely demolished the complex, with the exception of the tower itself. The keeper's dwelling was reconstructed, and a cypress wharf, 1,350 feet long, was added to the complex in 1898.

In the spring of 1952 the light was decommissioned; the radio beacon was moved to another site, and the tower itself was retained by the Coast Guard as a daybeacon for two years. Then on January 28, 1954, the land and improvements, including the tower, were transferred to the state of Louisiana for wildlife conservation purposes.

Red Fish Bar Light, Galveston Bay, Texas

Three lighthouses were established in Galveston Bay in 1854. Two were painted with red stripes, both marking dangerous shoals, and one was painted all white to mark the channel through the sand bar.

Red Fish Bar Light, white with red horizontal stripes, was effective both at night and as a daymark. The lamp, visible for ten miles, was thirty-five feet above sea level, and a large bell was used as a fog signal. The station was burned to the iron screw-piles during the Civil War and was not rebuilt and lighted again until May 8, 1868.

By 1894 the tiny light was almost useless as an aid to navigation. A cut had been dredged through the dangerous Red Fish Bar, out some distance from the light, and a light on the edge of the channel would have been of greater service. The old building was so decayed it could not be moved, so a new light, similar in construction to the old one, was built to mark the cut in 1900. It was kept in service until 1936, when a red skeleton tower went into service.

Aransas Pass Light, Texas

This brick lighthouse was built in 1855, but during the Civil War the Rebels destroyed the top twenty feet of the tower, along with the keeper's dwelling. It was completely rebuilt in 1867. A heavy screen is built around the light section of the tower to prevent birds from crashing into the glass.

THE WEST COAST, ALASKA, AND HAWAII

Point Loma Light, San Diego, California

The Old Point Loma Light, the southernmost of California's lighthouses and now a National Monument, was one of the first eight built in that state. Originally constructed to accommodate a lamp with a parabolic reflector, the lighthouse had to be altered even before it went into service, because the government was then beginning to use Fresnel lenses. That light was activated on November 15, 1855.

However, the lighthouse had been built on land so high—the light was 462 feet above sea level—that it was often obscured by low clouds. So a new tower (pictured here) was erected in 1891 on the tip of Point Loma just slightly above sea level.

Point Vincente Light, Los Angeles, California

This beautiful light station, constructed in the southern California Spanish style, was activated in 1926. The keeper's dwelling follows the style, with stucco walls and red tile roof. The tower is sixty-seven feet high and serves as a coastal light and a guide to Los Angeles Harbor.

Point Conception Light, Santa Barbara, California

Point Conception Light is another of the first eight original lighthouses in California. In order to be fitted with the new Fresnel lens, it had to be torn down and completely rebuilt before it had even been activated. It first saw service in February 1856; by 1875 the dwelling, atop which the light was situated, had settled and developed an irreparable crack. The replacement tower, pictured here, was built at a lower elevation in 1882; it is 133 feet above sea level and visible for twenty-six miles. It is basically inaccessible to the public.

Point Sur Light, Monterey, California

Constructed in 1889, this beautiful complex consists of a triple keeper's quarters, blacksmith/carpenter shop, oil house, fog-signal building, and the striking light tower. The keeper's quarters are located a block from the rest of the complex, and all of the original buildings are still intact. With the exception of the light tower and fog-signal building, the station is now under the jurisdiction of the California Department of Parks and Recreation.

The light was automated in 1972. It can be seen for twenty-five miles, and the radio beacon is effective in a fifty-mile radius. The original first-order Fresnel lens is now on display at the Alan Knight Museum in Monterey.

Point Pinos Light, Monterey, California

The second of the original eight lights built on the California coast, this lighthouse was constructed in 1855. It is one of three of the original eight still standing. The lighthouse survived the devastating earthquake of 1907 and is basically unaltered; the original Fresnel lens is still in good operating condition, and the lighthouse is today the oldest active light on the West Coast.

The light is under license to the city of Pacific Grove, which operates a museum there with period furniture and many historic lighthouse artifacts on display.

Yerba Buena Island Light, San Francisco, California

Built in 1875, this quaint Victorian tower has eight wooden sides. One of several lights marking San Francisco Bay, this light station originally had a steam-powered diaphone fog signal. The light has now been automated and is still active.

East Brothers Island Light, San Francisco, California

This light station on Point Richmond was constructed in 1874 and is one of the complexes built in the second phase of lighthouse building in California. It is one of seventeen erected in and around San Francisco Bay and is the oldest of this group still in operation.

Nominated to the National Register of Historic Places in 1969, East Brothers Light has been completely restored by a nonprofit organization formed in 1979 for the purpose of preserving the lighthouse for the benefit of the general public. It is now being operated as a bed and breakfast and is so popular that reservations need to be made months in advance. Its diaphone fog signal has been restored and is sounded occasionally for visitors.

Alcatraz Island Light, San Francisco, California

With the discovery of gold at Sutter's Mill in 1849, San Francisco became the hub of shipping in the area. In many cases the ships' crews joined the gold seekers, and soon the harbor was jammed with deserted vessels.

One of three lighthouses marking San Francisco Bay, the Alcatraz light was the first built on the West Coast—one of the original group of eight. Built in the Cape Cod style with the light tower thrust through the center of the keeper's dwelling, it was completed in 1854. In 1909 the old lighthouse was torn down to make way for a prison complex. A taller tower, illustrated here, was built at the same time, just outside the prison. The tower is eighty-four feet high but its focal plane, because of its location on the heights, is two hundred feet above the bay. Three sets of keeper's quarters are attached to the tower.

Point Bonita Light, Marin County, California

Put into commission on April 30, 1855, this lighthouse had the first fog signal on the West Coast—a cannon obtained from the Benicia Arsenal. During a heavy fog in 1855, the signal was operated continuously for three days and nights by one person, who got only two hours of rest during the entire time. Use of the cannon was discontinued in 1857, but the light is still active today.

As with the Point Loma lighthouse, the Point Bonita light was originally built on land so high it was frequently shrouded by the fog even when lower-lying land was clear. So a new lighthouse was built in 1877 at a lower elevation on "Land's End" at the western extremity of Point Bonita.

Point Reyes Light, California

Many vessels were wrecked on the finger of land that juts out into the Pacific at Point Reyes; to aid navigators in avoiding the hazard, this lovely sixteen-sided light was built in 1870. Although a nearby lighthouse is actually the working light, the original lamp in this lighthouse is occasionally turned on for visitors. The old engine building and an oil house remain. This complex is now under the jurisdiction of the National Park Service and is open to the public.

Cape Mendocino Light, California

This light was first put into commission in December 1868. By the following spring it had already begun to settle, and small cracks were appearing in the structure. Two years later an earthquake destroyed the keeper's dwelling but did not damage the tower. In 1873 another earthquake hit the area, opening a crack in the ground that ran almost up to the tower. The crack was filled with concrete, and despite subsequent attacks by nature, this tower still stands today.

Though the tower is only forty-three feet high, it is built on a promontory that puts the light 422 feet above sea level, making it the highest in the United States.

St. George Reef Light, Crescent City, California

The rocks and reefs around Point St. George are extremely dangerous. In 1865 the side-wheeler *Brother Jonathan* sank when it struck a ledge off the point. Two hundred fifteen passengers and crew were lost. However, it was not until 1881 that the Lighthouse Board decided to locate a light on these reefs—on Northwest Seal Rock off Point St. George. Due to delays in the appropriation of funds, and because of its exposed location on a rock six miles at sea, the lighthouse was ten years in the building, at a cost of $704,000—the most expensive lighthouse to that date. It was first lit on October 20, 1892.

Although at least one keeper has perished there in the rough seas, this granite lighthouse has withstood all the tortures to which nature has subjected it. Now abandoned, the light has been replaced with a lighted buoy.

Cape Blanco Light, Port Orford, Oregon

Constructed in 1870, this lighthouse was originally named Cape Orford Light; it is the most westerly light on the mainland of the United States. The fifty-nine-foot tower houses a 300,000-candlepower light that is 245 feet above sea level. The lighthouse is near Cape Blanco State Park and still beams its warning today.

Although the white-faced cliff had been known as Cape Blanco since 1603, it was being called Cape Orford at the time the lighthouse was being built, in an attempt to give the place an Anglo-Saxon name. The new appellation did not stick; by 1889 the Lighthouse Board was again calling it Cape Blanco.

Cape Arago Light, Coos Bay, Oregon

The original Cape Arago Light was established in 1866. The second lighthouse built on the Oregon coast, it was constructed on a rocky promontory that projected seaward from the location of the present lighthouse and was called Cape Gregory Light. Constant erosion by the sea led to the abandonment of the original lighthouse and the construction of the light at its present location in 1934.

Cape Arago Light, though primarily a coastal light, also marks the entrance to Coos Bay; it is situated on a small rocky island that is connected to the mainland by a narrow footbridge. The unmanned station has a powerful radio beacon, a fog signal, and an automated white light. Cape Arago Light is adjacent to Sunset Bay State Park.

Umpqua River Light, Reedsport, Oregon

Only after the local Indians had been fought off was this light station dedicated and lighted in 1857. Skirmish after skirmish occurred between the construction workers and the Indians. Only six years after construction the lighthouse was so threatened by erosion that the Lighthouse Board ordered removal of its lens. This had barely been accomplished when the lighthouse tumbled. A new light was not built at that location until 1894; it continues in operation today.

Cape Meares Light, Tillamook Bay, Oregon

Built in 1890, Cape Meares Light is five miles south of the entrance to Tillamook Bay and is within Cape Meares State Park. It is no longer active, having been replaced by an automated light and radio beam. A photomural display is now featured in the restored structure, which is open to visitors.

Point Robinson Light, Lower Puget Sound (Tacoma), Washington

This beautiful octagonal tower was originally established in 1855 as a fog signal station, equipped with a steam whistle. A light was added in 1857, and in 1915 the tower was raised to a height of forty feet above sea level. Built on an island, the light is accessible by ferry.

Alki Point Light, Seattle, Washington

A lighted navigational aid has been at this site for many years, though the date of establishment has not been recorded. In 1887 a wooden scaffold surmounted by a lantern was constructed on the site. Upgrading of the light became necessary with the increase in shipping, and the present structure was constructed in 1913.

One of Puget Sound's most tragic maritime disasters occurred off Alki Point in 1906 when the passenger steamer *Dix* collided with the steam schooner *Jeanie*, resulting in the loss of thirty-nine lives.

Point Wilson Light, Puget Sound (Seattle), Washington

Every mariner entering or leaving Puget Sound has to take Point Wilson into his reckoning if he does not wish to leave his vessel stranded on its sandy shores. When the weather is clear there is no problem, but in a dense fog there is a serious need for guidance. A lighthouse was constructed at the tip of Point Wilson in 1879, with a new concrete tower being built in 1914. In addition to the beacon, a deep-toned fog whistle became part of the warning system. However, even with the guidance of the light, the palatial coastal liner *Governor* collided with the freighter *West Hartland*, with a loss of eight lives just off Point Wilson Light on April 1, 1921.

Admiralty Head Light, Washington

Admiralty Head was early recommended as a site for a lighthouse. In 1858 the United States bought the land, and construction began immediately on the tower, which stood on the bluff. It was a low, white, square tower with a small lamp.

The United States fortified Admiralty Head in the 1890s; when Fort Casey was created, the old lighthouse had to go, as it stood on the most desirable spot for a battery of heavy guns. A new location for the light was procured within the grounds of the fort, and construction began in 1901. Eventually this lighthouse was declared surplus, and in 1941 the building was transferred to the War Department to be used for training activities. By 1955 this portion of Fort Casey became a state park, and the severely damaged old lighthouse building has since been restored to the way it appeared during the early part of the century.

Burrows Island Light, Burrows Island, Washington

Located on the western tip of the island from which it takes its name, this light station commands an area of treacherous currents. The light was established in 1906, as the only major aid to navigation in Rosario Strait and the Strait of Georgia. It is now operated as a fully automated, unmanned station.

Cape Hinchinbrook Light, Prince William Sound, Alaska

Marking the entrance to Prince William Sound, this light is one of Alaska's principal coast lights. Although the need for a lighthouse here was recognized as early at 1900, the light was not completed until November 15, 1910. Due to its high site, the lantern itself was 235 feet above sea level. The first fog signal was too weak, because of the dense fogs prevalent around the cape, and a more powerful signal was put into service in 1923.

A new concrete building with a sixty-seven-foot tower was built in 1934, when the cliffs beneath the original light (shown here) began to crumble. The old building was abandoned just in time, for its walls began to crack soon after. The newer light is situated well inland.

Cape Hinchinbrook Light not only marks the sound but also warns of the nearby Seal Rocks.

Molokai Light, Island of Molokai, Hawaii

This octagonal light tower, 138 feet tall, was constructed in 1909 on the north shore of the island. It is active today and carries a two-million-candlepower light. The tallest of the Hawaiian lights, it is reputed to be visible for twenty-eight miles under ideal conditions.

Makapuu Point Light, Island of Oahu, Hawaii

Makapuu Point Light is one of the most important aids to navigation in the Hawaiian Islands. Established in 1909, it is a landfall light for vessels bound from the United States, Mexico, and Central America. In 1927 a radio beacon was added, with two eight-foot antennas carrying the signals. The concrete tower, at only forty-six feet high, is just large enough to accommodate the necessary lighting apparatus. A taller tower is not needed here, as the lighthouse is located on a rugged headland 420 feet above the sea.

The hyper-radiant lens installed in the tower is one of the world's most brilliant. It is eight and one-half feet wide, thirteen feet high, and is made up of 1,140 prisms of French-made polished glass. It is fitting that in Hawaiian *makapuu* means "bulging eye."

Diamond Head Light, Honolulu, Island of Oahu, Hawaii

This lighthouse can be seen on the southwest side of the extinct Diamond Head volcano. Originally constructed in 1899 and rebuilt in 1917, this light is surpassed in longevity only by the Aloha Tower and Barbers Point lights. Diamond Head Light is one of the better-known beacons in Hawaii and stands as a sentinel to Honolulu Harbor, flashing a welcome to mariners arriving from east or west.

The present concrete structure was built in 1917 and is about fifty-five feet tall. Through the years this lighthouse has been modernized and is today fully automated. The light can be seen for eighteen miles. Diamond Head Light is presently the quarters of the Commander of the Fourteenth Coast Guard District.

Kilauea Point Light, Island of Kauai, Hawaii

Made of concrete slightly tapering at the top, this lighthouse was established in 1913. It is perched on a breathtakingly beautiful promontory overlooking the sea, on land owned by the Kilauea Sugar Company. Kilauea Point Light is the western counterpart of Makapuu Point Light, serving as the landfall light for ships coming from the Orient.

The first-order Fresnel lens installed in the light was of a modified clamshell shape—reputedly costing $12,000—one of the largest of its type in the Pacific. With an oil lamp the lens afforded a flash of 240,000 candlepower; when electrified, the 1,000-watt lamp was estimated to equal 4.5 million candlepower.

In 1976 a light beacon was constructed adjacent to Kilauea Point Light, which was then decommissioned. Today, operating nearly twenty-four hours a day, a powerful radio beacon sends out its signals from Kilauea Point.

THE GREAT LAKES

Outer Island Light, Apostle Islands (Duluth), Minnesota

One of several serving the area, this lighthouse was established in 1874 in response to increased shipping activity at the west side of Lake Superior. Once the railroad had reached Duluth, the town became a bustling port with need for safe ship passage in darkness and foggy weather.

Duluth North Pier Light, Duluth, Minnesota

Begun in 1909, this lighthouse was finished in 1910 at a cost of only $4,000. The tower stands thirty-seven feet high, and the focal plane of the light is forty-three feet above water level. There are two other lights in the immediate area.

Wind Point Light, Racine, Wisconsin

Established on the lower west short of Lake Superior in 1880, this 108-foot cylindrical white tower flashes a light that can be seen for twenty-nine miles. The light was electrified in 1924, and in 1964 it was entirely automated. The keeper's dwelling, once inhabited by the keeper and two assistants, was turned over to the town of Wind Point to be used as a town hall. It is surrounded by a lovely park.

Michigan Island Light, Wisconsin

Found in the Apostle group of islands in Lake Superior, the Michigan Island lighthouse was built in 1857 and last rebuilt in 1930. The tower itself is 102 feet high, but because of its location, the light is 170 feet above the water and can be seen for eleven miles.

Chicago Harbor Light, Illinois

Marking the entrance to Chicago Harbor from Lake Michigan, this lighthouse sits on the northern arm of the outer breakwater. Originally built in 1893, the lighthouse was moved to its present location in 1919. It has a brick-lined cast-iron tower, eighteen feet in diameter, and is still in operation.

The lens installed in Chicago Harbor Light was originally intended for the Point Loma lighthouse in California. But the lens was so admired by the Lighthouse Board that they delayed its installation in order to exhibit it at the Paris Exhibition and then the Chicago Exposition of 1891; it won prizes at both places. By the time the Chicago Exposition closed, another lens had been found for Point Loma and the award-winning lens was installed in the Chicago Harbor lighthouse instead.

Rock of Ages Light, Isle Royale, Michigan

Though situated in Lake Superior, much closer to the Minnesota shore (and the Canadian province of Ontario), Isle Royale is nonetheless part of the state of Michigan. Located on the island, and put into service in 1908, is Rock of Ages Light. The tower is built of brick on a concrete foundation. The lens is 117 feet above lake level and guides vessels past the shoals around the island, especially those ships bound to and from Duluth, Minnesota. The lighthouse is especially valuable during storms, when ships travel in the lee of Isle Royale rather than risk the southerly and rougher course.

Still in service, this lighthouse is viewed every year by visitors to Isle Royale National Park.

Stannard Rock Light, northeast of Marquette, Michigan

Spectacularly located on Stannard Rock Shoal in Lake Superior, this lighthouse is forty-five miles northeast of Marquette and twenty-five miles southeast of Manitou Island. It was established in 1882.

This isolated, gray conical tower is truly subjected to the ravages of nature, but it is still in operation, standing 102 feet above the water. Its light, automated in 1961, can be seen for eighteen miles.

While the station was being automated in 1961, a propane-gas explosion killed one Coast Guardsmen and seriously injured two others. Much of the equipment in the lower portions was destroyed, and the light went out, but it was two days before the tragedy was reported.

Stannard Rock is the lighthouse most distant from shore anywhere in this country and is known as "the loneliest place in America."

Big Bay Point Light, Marquette, Michigan

This lighthouse was authorized by Congress in 1893 and was completed at a cost of $25,000 in 1896. It is a two-story building of brick construction. The tower rises from the middle of the eighteen-room keeper's dwelling and reaches a height of 105 feet. Having been sold in 1928, the lighthouse is no longer in operation. It had been under the jurisdiction of the Coast Guard but is now a popular bed and breakfast inn.

Grand Traverse Light (Cat's Head Point), Michigan

Built in 1858 near the end of a long arm of land that separates Grand Traverse Bay from the rest of Lake Michigan, this light tower extends from the roof of a two-story keeper's dwelling. When the Coast Guard built a nearby steel skeletal tower with an automatic light in 1972, the old lighthouse was abandoned and is now a part of Michigan's Leelanau State Park.

Old Mission Point Light, Traverse Bay, Michigan

Although Congress appropriated money to construct this lighthouse on Lake Michigan in 1859, it wasn't completed until 1870, delayed by the Civil War. The lighthouse was built at the end of the scenic peninsula dividing the West Arm from the East Arm of Grand Traverse Bay. The structure still stands, now the property of the State of Michigan. The lens was removed in 1933.

Old Mission Point Light is almost exactly on the forty-fifth parallel, halfway between the Equator and the North Pole.

St. Martin's Reef Light, near Mackinac Strait, Michigan

Established in 1927, this lighthouse is located adjacent to St. Martin Island in Lake Huron about eight miles directly north of Mackinac Island. The focal plane of the light is sixty-five feet above the water.

Tawas Light, Saginaw Bay, Michigan

About 1854, a lighthouse was built at the entrance to Saginaw Bay on the opposite side from the Point aux Barques lighthouse, which was built in 1848. Sand-laden currents gradually extended the point further out into Lake Huron, and twenty years later, the light stood a mile from the end of the point. The lighthouse shown here was built in 1877 at the new end of the point.

This area of Michigan is referred to as the "Cape Cod of the Midwest."